AFTER THESE MESSAGES
Sean Cole

AFTER THESE MESSAGES
Sean Cole

LUNAR CHANDELIER PRESS

2022

Cover: "48" by Barbara Price, 2021
Copyright © 2022 by Sean Cole

AUTHOR'S NOTE

In February 2009, I started writing poems while watching TV commercials. That is, whenever I was watching TV anyway, I'd pick up my notebook during the commercials and just start riffing off of what was happening on the screen. (The Oscars were especially productive. They're long. Plus there are a lot of irresistibly silly trailers for action movies.)

Sometimes I'd incorporate the advertising patois that works its way under your brain-skin after a few listens. But mostly I just responded to what I saw, which was America in all of its aspirational, contradictory glory. Often the ads would breach the TV glass and blend in with whatever was happening in my life at the time. Hence, a lot of the poems turned into the kind of first-person, fever dreams you have when your fever is caused by eating too much spicy food before bed. There I was – consorting with celebrities, sampling various products that weren't intended for me, and exalting myself in a way that bespoke a deeply problematic character flaw. It was fun.

I started looking forward to my favorite shows the way I used to look forward to a good stretch of dedicated writing time – or at least I felt a lot less guilty about parking myself on the couch for several hours. Also, I found that I would pay more attention to the commercials than I did to the shows. To this day, when I'm puttering around the apartment with the TV on, I'll catch myself standing frozen in front of the screen during the ads, and then walking off to wash the dishes when they're over. Commercials are like poems in a few ways. They can be addictive. Consuming them doesn't take a great deal of time. Creating them means squeezing an awful lot of persuasion into a limited space. Looking back at the poems, you can kind of guess which demographic the show, and its advertisers, are targeting – young or old, affluent or not, majority male or female, how much of what kind of food they might eat, what their values might be. What clearly unites all of these demographics, what unites us as Americans, is that we all wish to retain our college weight while consuming large quantities of snack food, beer, and analgesics, and driving at speeds not recommended by the American Automotive Association.

I thought I'd try to fill an entire book with only these poems. But then I thought, no. They should work the way commercials do: as interstitial featurettes of their own, punctuating the action of what you're actually choosing to view. I did keep track, mostly, of what I was watching when I wrote a given poem, and the date. I decided to leave that information off and let the commercial poems stand on their own. I've left out a few of them just via the kind of quality control you always do when putting together a collection like this.

Many thanks to the journals and presses who published some of these poems in the past: Black Clock, Court Green, Shampoo, Boog Literature, Edgar and Lenore's Publishing House, Dusie, and Pressed Wafer. I also want to thank David Kirschenbaum for always urging me to write, Aaron Kiely for being my bon homie, and William Corbett for his patience, thoughtful curation, and for generally being a hugely copasetic daddy-o.

To my mother Patricia Clark, 1934 - 2015
and to William Corbett, 1942 - 2018

VERILY

O Lord in heaven migrating south –
thou art curious why I use the formal
pronoun for you. You is wondering
why I bother using any word:
you're a bird.

POEM FOR BILLY JOEL

I did happen to start the fire actually – ripped a bunch of rumpled
information from the pile beside the nostril in my house. I'm lucky.
No New York apartment has an analogue invector like this, which is why
all the nimrods in your music keep breaking up with each other.
Up Hudson-way, where nimrods get divorced, is Storm King Mountain.
It stretches for a cold cloud. So moronic. "Storm King"
is a type of furnace after all. We learn this from the combo
"New Radiant Storm King" on whose albums all connubiality
remains in tact. You could learn a thing or two from them
Mr. Hicksville. Farther north are two abutting towns what cuddle out
the frozen latitude. New Radiance, they're called, and Storm King, no
kidding. Weirdly, out in Colorado a whole other mountain called Storm King
caught fire in 1994. It understood the meaning of its name.
I know the meaning of my name, Sean Cole. It means
"God is swarthy." Your name, on the other hand, means "Condom Jehovah."
I say this not to "front on you" as the idiom goes (hence "cold front" hence
"cold snap" hence "oh snap" hence "damn that shit is cold.") No.
I say this to disarm the dedomiciling bomb of your baleful lyric, Mr. Joel.
I beg you: tear down this Italian restaurant.

POSTCARD TO DECEMBER

You'd like it here it's cold. The freaking house. Without plans, I've come to resemble a doorknob curled in the loose grass. Been one hill of a year: born in Africa, clowned up with divorce. A close friend said I saved his life but I didn't notice. A gorgeous lawyer says "I love you" to my new clone each night. Empty sets of clothes milk up the floor. And yet I'm dumb. Snowed shut. Clued out. The jump-gun closes my hand sometimes. Things'll be all right. I'll clean the rug – learn the capitals of states – gain new insights via booze. The reason you've been old so long is that you don't die. Now and then you fade in, I ask you stuff, you say "ouch."

COMMERCIAL BREAK

I don't have rheumatoid arthritis. I do have
a special plastic spout my girlfriend gave me
to keep wine fresh. She's gone now. All
is loss. I'm the next Dancing With Stars
champion, though, so that keeps me going.
This place stinks of absentia. What happens
when my own house reminds me of us,
my own skin. My "a-ha" moment
is still in the future. Fortunately,
I've found the most effective yogurt
for my hair. Potent, proven, leave it in
long enough it becomes cheese. That's when Sean's
ready for dating. Five years ago,
a message was buried in the fashion world.
They said we should wait. That message
is me. Take a picture.
Send it to someone you love.
Forget she'll eventually leave.
Rub all over with cranberry soap.
Repeat.

POEM FOR OLIVER WENDELL HOLMES

It's cool to be from Boston – a place where you can say
"Trust me, I have no fuckin' clue," and mean it. Hustle out
folded street-car to snow bank, drop dull money into coffee cup,
George Washington coquettish Man-a-Lisa on your dollar dollar. I'm so
gay-Bostonian monkish in this hubris hovel. One man circling five
rooms on the phone saying "no" to his Boss Angeles over and over. It's so
huge to go to the hospital you were born in, have your finger sutured. Radiator
bottles clang together in the belfry, the knelling pulls my Fridays open.
Goddamn, it's Thursday, I'm on all these Canadian drugs. I'm in Boston.
Tiny grisly men with paint jobs circle the graveyard. "Look at Paul
Revere in his brief cocoon," they say. "That's not him. That's not
dangerously Santa Claus over by the maple, that's not Mother Goose
dead there in the dirt – dirty dead woman imposter poet of bunchy hymns,
it's someone else." O Boston. Home of cinnamon mobsters. A snow cone
walks the canal here, marries a tug boat. We all waggle boxer shorts
through the window confessional. O you pretty babe in high hat babcock.
My city. Farthing for your hardly able-bodied thought-control.

MARCH

> *"E"; you know what "E" means.* – Jaime Saenz

Well this doesn't look good does it. Squirreling
lotion and tissues into the bedroom with me. Really
my hands are cracked. And the Kleenex should be
bedside, it's where the sad happens. Who am I afraid
of scandalizing? Santa? I live like a spit
in a bay: surroundless.

Sure – she took the HER out of HERE, leaving E.
Jaime Saenz said "you know what 'E' means" but I don't.
Stick it on its side and shut the window.
Origami is everything to the singleton.

To build birds. That's what capital "He" does. You won't be
solo with enough paper, this form of life needs property.
Prop. To prop up. To stick a wood sword under a beached
boat, let a crab crawl under. Oh Christ, fold me. I'm banging
around this house like a bee in a bell. Ringing zilch.

APRIL FIRST

As though I asked about your family.
I don't care who you call. You could call
Florence Henderson for all I care.
Call her hair. Her Brady bob. That blonde
glib mop, flopped across the mouth bell.
I'm writing this on the back of a cell bill.
It used to be a short poem.
Now it's a villanelle – one from hell
where no verb echoes. Your voice
lost in the dead hollow of a jail.

I know the girl who designed the Verizon logo.
For real.
She's a woman now
named Jen. Once

she called me a Martian lecher leper.
That's not so.
She never called me.
And for that I've kept her
endlessly esteemed.

COMMERCIAL BREAK

Diet Coke will make you fit
in that red dress and give
to the poor. It will also
make you gay and famous.
If you drink Tide
you'll die. I'm hugely
lucky. I work at home
and am hereby reminded
I'm lucky. I'm also
divorced, which means
I'm an adult type of dead.
Onyx cut-out city on violet sky.
Audi: make me a tractor I can
carve questions in the yard with.
Twin suns examine my lunch
with Sherlock things. Two pennies
make the tiniest monocles.
I'm allergic to harm. Take
this pill despite dry mouth,
hump-back, aggressive fatness
and helium spine. Can't I drink
as much as I want and still stay
hard and charming? When a cute
Chinese child takes a digital picture
it's magic. I think I'm in love with
being this thin and blonde. All
the boys in shorts automatically
read my mail. Even if I mailed
them a Coke they'd read the label.
Your dad always told me you were
my sister. But I didn't know
how much you ate. I'm glad I'm
thinner than you. That my computer
is smaller. That I'm Holly Hunter.
That I'm a brilliant meteorologist.
The world's nations battle over my
saliva. The Coke I drink today
sews the seeds of democracy.
I heart that.

PROSE FOR SHARON MESMER

for Sharon Mesmer

Sharon Mesmer you're related to Franz Mesmer from where we get the word "Mesmerize" I was right. I write that I was right because I'm glad about it. That and I'm a calligraphic sex-dentist chewing a train. My name's so long it's like Sharon Mesmer's name written 40 times for 40 nights every hour to "infernity." Infernal night-carrot I blog about how good for my vision you are. The way I drive is abominable as I'm writing this while driving dazzled by the opposing beams. Big boobs of illumination like Sharon's. Her headlights I mean. Her car's beams – don't go dirty on me I'll girl-fight you. O Franz Mesmer you invented Sharon. You also touted magnetism: a revolution as salubrious as Advil replacement. You and followers magnetized trees, turned them into magnetism ATM machines. A boy touched a tree and shook but the boy didn't exist. Only his commander existed. His bank commander, barking at him, "Boy I'll hold your feet until you tremble and then abandon you!" This man was his dad. His name was Ben (the man). His name was "Bad Ben I'll Get You Back" Jackson. He had two nicknames: "Nick" and "I'll Get You Back Times a Billion." What do you call Nick when he's been nasty? I call him "cock." I literally know a guy named Nick van der Kolk whom I call "van der Pussy" when I'm mad, that's not very poetic, he likes it. No one knows this poem's being written at the moment not even Sharon. Not Nick. Not Bad Ben and definitely not Franz Mesmer who's dead. Died of lying to people. Lied so long his tongue evolved into a flute. He lay in the ground looking lovely, as long as "lovely" means "not living anymore." Now his life is just a tall tale I tell in poems dedicated to his septuagint: Sharon.

MONTHIVERSARY

Somewhere dear, sheer summer freaks on without us. Such a time
machine I've climbed into, banyan syrup seeping from my
bat mask. Somewhere, pure eagles share their lunches
with each other. Massachusetts shares its lunch with New Hampshire
in summer. Brotherhood is easy above 70 degrees. When your bike
careens into September, you enter bother-hood. That's no good.
A blood cloud bursts with ice inside it. Right now I'm staring down
an ice goat. Not an animal but an actual iceman made of goat. It's
right there where Lowell and Summer streets converge.
I could sing to you about this but I'd rather sing about porch
bells gathering their pennies together. Somewhere, pointy horse
music steals into the reeds, O friend of August, you don't know what
it means to watch such music goad itself along for no reason.
What is the opposite of an ice queen? I'd call you it, sitting
in my ice truck. I'd call you "angel" if I hadn't already. I know!
I'll call you Snowy Urola – a moth the length of an oak leaf. It floats
from green to green: mum. Why say anything this engineless
morning? I'll sing. I'll share my five-months-ago lunch with you,
beautiful habit. I'll lean in and brush the salt off of your green lunch.
I'll rub these sandwiches together to make music we can climb into
like a July balloon. Oh man what savage music I could conjure
with this summer mood I've imagined.

GANSETT POINT

You're an egg-making machine,
Mayim, your name means "water"
in Hebrew. You're slight, and ropey,
a slew of cantaloupe slices in cream
would feed you. "Slew" as in we
slew the cantaloupe with off-handed spleen
and set it in a bowl, laid the eggs you made
atop it – two troubled frog's eyes in a yellow
dream. Drawn with food. We're humans
born from lima beans inside a stove.
To hew to social norms isn't like us:
we eat the eggs and melon with a green
spoon, not a blue one.

After lunch,
you swim with Sue, your mom, I walk
the opposite direction and somehow
hit the water too. The water, Mayim,
it's all around us – temperate, see-through
and saline. Walker, Kailey, Des and I read
separate cups of tea leaves where the boats array.
The rhythmic hitting of the dock against the beam.
Somewhere, in distant lawn,
a grub crawls on a leaf. It doesn't know
its integers, nor fractals, its esteem
is low. Still it shoulders through the grass,
eating things that grubs delight to eat.

The mirror has my father's legs.
You've got Sue, your mother's, teeth.
These eggs are better than the ones I do.
The yolks are protein moons against two clouds.
Sometimes in Tel Aviv they do a dance.
It's called "Mayim Mayim."
I don't know how it goes.
It's wet though – like a stream.
Streams don't have names like creeks do.
Which seems unjust. Also,
Greeks have names. There's one called
Doug Cole whom I'm related to.
He's half Greek, and half asleep on
Dramamine. His home's a boat. It sits

there in the archive pool, a sloop,
it's hull as bare as bird feet in a stew.

Tonight I'll eat a sandwich on a hill.
The sun will bow, the moon will join
its team. I'll stand between them, unsure
who is who. The bay will cow its orphan
dial tone. Let's have a toast. Not a speech
but heated bread inside a glass. One slice.
It's hard to eat like that, let's lay it flat
and place two eggs across it. One for you,
Mayim, and one for Sue, and me. That's
three. Crack another in the pan and cover
with the glass pan mask oh good you did.
One cool heart opened here's gold inside
and albumin. Same protein as in our
blood. We're each a flood contained
within a shell -- an orange fallen
from a tree that somehow,
against all pauses, grew.

COMMERCIAL BREAK

Madam I'm animated.
My 401k this summer
is wholly invested in beer, candy bars,
and bay windows.
For $125 a month this month,
you can look outside –
watch your friend John
on the lawn
pretend to time travel.

The future is so damn sex-addicted.
Bodies in motion. Bodies
summering inside themselves –
smashing cantaloupe.
Bite sized fruit.
The world gets small as a grape
under scrutiny.
Love means making
that jogging meeting
with your hot fiancé.
On the way to Denny's
you talk about work.
Your thumbs trip over each other's
assets. Your future child asks
how are you changing the environment? Clearly,
neon is out. But taut
medicine ball obliques
are in. Work them en route
to the oyster bar
for a Lime-Weiser.

POEM FOR PUSSIES

You stupid leopard. You,
lazing there reading Whitman
between naps like a pied spud. What spot
is this the rogue one on your hip that
doesn't tap the rhythm of your coat?
Brain of a star fruit. Yet
lithe enough to duck poachers.
How's it done, falsehood?
How've you lulled the jungle into
shameless flirts? What's the future
of a slouch like you? Roaming
in and out of myth, wedding no one?
Newsprint-smeared nose growing
spiteless? Mostly, it's pity
hangs my shirt up in your wardrobe.
Speckless life is yours, yet you
pick brindle.

TIGER

Tiger says "I'll tear your new orifice" with his eyes. Ire.
Iger plus "N" is the river I send my hate across to evade
his name shame. Middle is "grr," a gerund with fur.
I'm a jungle neophyte. The height I leap transforms air to stair.
To err is human, but it's tiger too. If only I could undo
his receptor, unglue the high gloss in his roaring ogle.
Once, I was mammalian. Now I race through past eras, aping.

HOMEWORK

Walking over Gowanus canal I feel relieved
not to be lying face down in it. It's 3rd Street.
Home of the sun. And I've just landed on this
water lily and am not bad looking yet and don't know
I will one day know you and later not know you.
Fabulous days in New York are boring and unrelatable.
They involve booze often but the awful ones do too.
I'm dictating this into a text function which replaced
the word "booze" with "boobs." Ditto those, I guess.
Ditto the silence that grows when you
close your eyes outside in the morning.

The day I'm talking about had a warehouse in it.
Also a printing press the height of a small judge.
Aaron and Sharon were there comparing biceps.
Their names rhyme a little. Wine
fell out glass bottles into tapered plastic.

The day I met you was night. We were drunk.
It felt fated, though now our offices are three
Chelsea blocks apart and every day is a thin
ruse. After meeting was months before the sun
came out, months before we watched it set
from the bar above the grocery store above
Gowanus. Who builds a gourmet food emporium
over a superfund site? Who says "no"
to your whole face which is so pliable?

I thought a little about cities the other day –
how no two ever make a baby city.
They don't blend. They just relentlessly
border each other – lying still
on either side of a forgotten treaty.
Every day lies next to the next one,
they don't speak. They're divided
by the honey pill between seconds.
Two people don't describe their days,
they sit on opposite ends of a table.
Describe a day – you're given another
to compare it to. Better to let it lie,
like a foundry crumbling beside a well –
that humble and sun-stained.

COMMERCIAL BREAK

An historic day.
The day I shove a battle of cheese
down your gullet. The day my ex-
lover calls me "productive."
In the jar museum
I bizarre a tiny missile at your
bite-size cowboy. I pour
ice-cold coffee on your sand
piazza. "This cinnamon twist

was rubbed all over your ex's
breasts," said the man in the beer
speedo. That made me acid. Summer
starts in 3-times-3 days. That's
when 2 swords cross, 2 jagged
bottle edges engage, sloughing reason.
"Shit, there ain't a waterboardable
offense more badass than smothering
your own mother with a square of Velveeta."
The glorious Knievel stand-in said that.
I load another Cheeto in the face-eraser, yelling
"Orange!"

BIRTHDAY ACROSTIC

May she-poems resplendent in draped reeds
alight your shoulders. Talcum for their feet.
Remorse departs your red calculator in shards. Jean
Kirkpatrick patted me on the back

last week saying "Oh, sorry, I thought you were Mark."
Am amorous of you Lamoureux, by
magnitudes. Hills of admiration
outfit my township. Were I
Uri Geller you'd be ferried from here in a
rick-shaw of hot spoons, your inner lunar
eclipse removed like a birthmark.
Um, congratulations on your birth, Mark – its anniversary.
X marks it. A kiss on your crown part.

BIRTHDAY ACROSTIC

Elephants can't remember shit; it's a damn lie. I'd use a cuss more pointed than "damn" but I'm an elephant so none occurs. I used to soup around in a reservoir of words – scoop them with my hose-nose and textify my scalp. Sorrily now, the Africa of my vocab goes underemployed. (Can't even remember which letter rejoinders "vocab" is it "u?" Ah, is it you. Such an inquest. Is it you who'll deem me braver than the eagle desert? Is it you who'll save me from the

hook brow of myself – is it you who already did?) Kid, my fears are infinite. All they meant was an elephant never forgets anything bad. He regrets. Conserve your pity though. I'm no pea, shrieking at the bottom of a bowl of kelp. (I don't even know what kelp is. I'm a land mammal.) No recall is an eloquence of its own. I can't prove this. Come. Sit here near the new tree root of my cerebrum. We'll pass an even grayness back and forth like old soldiers.

BIRTHDAY ACROSTIC

Poems are such boring little disasters. Take this one: the least
eruptive Redoubt. Every terra fissure measures better. No
Japan ever melted via poem. You can't crush a hoem unless you're
Kenward Elmslie. Holy Iceland I'm bored as honey already. (Sigh.)

Maybe I'm a Dane. Maybe I'm an aimless Dane who doesn't countenance
avalanches. Not poem ones. All this April I've craved May, pedaling the
L train myself. Brown outs grinding the wires of words quiet. Sighing (see above).
I fell in love with an idiot cyclone before – a poet. She wasn't
Nagasaki. I needed Nagasaki to get me from love to forever. Finally I
opened her mail. Hail fell out. The floor was all marbles and ball bearings.
"Vote me out of the grove" she said, so I did. And I've never felt,
since then, that a bit of poesy could destroy you. Sure, there's
Kenward, sure. Beyond him, there is only actual snow, and rabies, also
Ireland (I'm worried about Ireland and its squalls) oh and there's New York.

COMMERCIAL BREAK

Gene Simmons: you relentless sugar addict.
You are not a doctor. You're a black and white
horror movie about rain. I scream,
you scream – you throw
my TV in the trash.   We

are as little children biting sugar cane.

Now we're at the man salon denuding our nickels.
I mean knuckles. I mean we're murdering our friends,
laying money on their eyes. This
is a hot world. So much speed
and then lunch. Then, lean on my phone
until Gene calls to upset my daughter.

UNION STREET

I bet it's fashionable to be this lonely.
Lips shellacked into a bum-out rictus.
They'll want me on screen. Like James
Dean. But not as deceased. I was
in a movie about driving once and
adultery. A famous woman in denim
attempted to blow her former husband
back into love with her it was cluelessly
sad. I wasn't the husband -- I played
an arm-rest. The radio's disconsolate
tonight. People on it imitating a hail
storm. I can feel the weight of this
whole high-rise as I lean out of its sill
smoking. Still smoking. Concrete
and brick with thick steel running
through its middle. Someone lives
up on the roof above me in a boxy
crow's nest growing food in short
buckets and tubs. I can't imagine
anything lonelier than their row
of shoes right inside the door
to everywhere. A shoe
is lonely. A pair is a possible
vacation somewhere. But climb
into those sneakers and where
do you go really? Find out what's
playing at the movie place where
they serve booze? Glide through
six orange train stops to the wine
house you turned your ex's best
friends onto?   Yes.
I'm at a table there now.
This poem's a travel poem.
All poems are. All people
are astronauts orbiting a short star,
being orbited by their infernal
ruminant. Years aren't very long
anymore. This past one
put me into effing Jason
Robards boots of self-abuse. A dude
at the next table just said "That's
literally my best idea." People talk

that way. Lovers pass the windows
of this bruise-hall, peering in
to make me crownless. They pause
to kiss in full view as if throwing
the switch on a hurt-throne. Everyone's
around me. Their eye-horizons rise
to meet the body cumulus.
The school across the street still
speaks quietly through its red doors.

INDEX

    for Zachary Schomburg

I'm getting work done.
Drinking is a kind of work.
Everybody grims his eyebrows at
the brown table, grinning effort.
I don't know what there is to smile about. Wine
is the juice of dirt.
No girl pairs to the one I threw
golf balls at the bar with.
We re-ruined this glass town.
We made straw homes collapse.
Once, we paired a half-house with its mirrorer.
That was hot. "Shake hands with me,"
I said to her, "Let's sleep a little in a cab."
She said things too. Brown things.

POEM

for Russell and Norabelle

I went to Denmark. It was dark. "Babump" our plane
landed. All the Danes yelled "ooch!" and rolled over. It's a nation of acute
reflexes. I went there for eleven hours, long enough
to watch the sky rise over the bike arrivals and drive past the palace
on the postcard of Copenhagen in Denmark where I've landed, "babump,"
successfully. First time someone's held a sign with one of my names
on it. He leads me to a fancy car parked in the car park here
in Denmark; they say "car park" here just like in England I know it.
We ride a Danish mile into town which is nine kilometers. I'm ready
to survey Copenhagen with all its rain huts. I think a river runs
beside it. If I'm not mistaken a bus lane only for buses abuts
the shriek of people biking down their dedicated Dane corral.
I mean "shriek" like a blue or yellow sweep of color on thick
fabric -- unedgeful on its sides. The whole encounter
with Denmark is like that and Copenhagen is its messenger.
I buy a big hotel then sell it back; eleven hours isn't long enough
to make a buck that way. The hotel's called Phoenix, like the bird. I burn
it down. It springs back from the earth like a grapevine,
higher than it was. The entire basement contains my friend
Jonathan Menjivar, plus giant lemon danish and a cold egg.
"Hey," I say in Danish which is "hi." "Huh?" he says. "I need
to bathe," I say, "Can I use your basic bathroom that they
gave you? Can you Copenhagen with that?" It's the first time
he's seen my shirt off. And it's in Denmark! There are bicyclists
here which are rain droplets clinging to a green bell.
We have to go to Odense which both my Danish
friends say I'm saying wrong. There's a festival in Denmark,
in Odense. It's about Jonathan and me and other things.
It's about work. Which in Danish sounds like "fow," spelled "f-a-g."
So on paper it looks like the "Fagfestival." That never gets
less funny to Jonathan and me because we're man-children.
Another fancy car collects us up like a dark frog electing flies
into its gut. That's what elections are like in Denmark they're
1) wet and 2) destructive. We ride for half an hour, and then
another half an hour and another. A woman who wins
things by photographing them is with us. I wish she didn't
hail from Winnipeg -- it's triggering. Everyone in Denmark
watches as we trail a lonely bicyclist from one dumb hamlet
to another. It's leveling in a discommodious fashion but that's
Denmark for you. Petrol flows from liter bottles at roadside

grow houses. Chocolate eggs with toys inside them wrapped
in foil fall out of chocolate hens. The Fagfestival's in full effect
when we get there. James Carville is sitting on a couch.
That's not part of the poem, it's just a fact. His hairless cranium
irradiates my blood Cassandras. Jonathan and I look Danish
on stage if you gauge by how the audience is dressed.
We're like a fly flexing in a mirror. A girl in the back writes
"this is so great" in her gray notebook and then erases it.
The world is Danes. And Denmark is the dirt carapace that
curls toward Danish ocean. We regret nothing. We're pure
as Denmark's firm terra deepening in ground blossom.

COMMERCIAL BREAK

Monday,
Charles Barkley comes to download music with me.
We'll sit in each other's warmth, the lithium of beef
inducing lewdness.

I'm a PC. Charles
is allergic to falafel.

Together, maybe a casino. Then bed.

Perchance I'll purchase the next boudoir
set before election season. I'm so
not looking forward to the next
president. My honeymoon persists just
five weeks into this fire sale.

Let's go someplace. Hurt some folks.
Say Bono did it.

Charles, how about that?

My new tattoo is of you.
I'm the largest family I know. Emailing
myself with amazing concision.
I'll buy diamonds, pretend Charles
did it, look at all the women's backs
in Manhattan, pretend they're yours.

CROSSING MONITOR

Don't wear socks on your hands.
Your pants will leap at them – the hem.
Your plans will melt. Who wants melted
plans? Back before the lava stiffened
all was flood. A Hudson earth – no
shale filling tributary, no pulling shale
into the sands. No hands.
                              Dear:
who thought of everything?
It was the horse. Look at the dirt.
The motor of this globe is leg.
Every variant a long stilt; even
vegetation trails from stem.
Please don't claim opposable triumph all
the time; it's tribusive.
Don't tell your shirk what your yearn is doing.
Don't fly off to cleat rafter either –
that's just mocking presagacity.
And for garden's sake, my beautineer,
stop wearing socks on your hands.

TO ACROPOLIS

There's no marathon like the Boston Marathon 'cause the Boston Marathon
ends at a library. If you try changing Boylston from three lanes to four there
a bus will veer and lift your Geo Prizm in the air, I've tried it.
Driver's side-mirror bursts in gemmy disco. I had a crush
on a girl when I was 9, thrust a nervous ring into her fist, the kind
that comes in bubble plastic. She shrugged. You would too
if I was 9 and gave you costume rubies. That was in a Massachusetts
town God made by neglecting a lake. Eight years later
I dry-humped my study partner in a phone booth outside
Boston Library where the Marathon ends.

The Grecian Marathon never ceases 'cause it's a town. Pheidippides
ran from there to Athens and dropped dead. But not before reporting
Greece beat Persia at The Battle of Marathon. He was the earliest
journalist. Also called a hemerodrome. Also a herald. Courier.
Day-runner. Day-long runner. Day-long running courier. Or
professional day-long running courier. Nude in a nineteenth
century work by Luc-Olivier Merson declaring "we won."
Collapse at the sandal straps of the frizzling crowd, Pheidippides,
you've done your historializing.

Johnny Kelley's spirit died on Heartbreak Hill in 1936
when a native named Tarzan passed him. I like that story. Both
because an Indian won the Boston race that year and it means
the "Heartbreak" part isn't literal. I thought they called it that
'cause someone had an infarction but no. Bostonians
can analogize in the legends we relay occasionally.
I'm an eighth native. Don't know which nation but I hope
it's the same as Tarzan's. Ellison Myers "Tarzan" Brown
is in your town, Boston, you'd better laurelize him.

"Are you all right?" people call and ask even though
I don't live in Boston anymore. That's the difference
between it and here. New York's a place you leave
and never were. Boston you've never left it once
you're gone. "Yes I'm fine," I say into the phone, "everyone
I know is still alive." In my glimmer, the whole city's
crumbled to the Charles, the sun concussing in its shards.
Growing up in Boston means to damn your constant
rearview yearn across the Atlantic. You bring that with
you – that return. Return. A world of it. It's all right.
Everything finishes when it does, and the night ends,
and eventually will restart.

COMMERCIAL BREAK – TORONTO

What is fun?
Nearly being maimed in a cold-water obstacle course?
Drawing a man's face on my back during home restoration?
I hurt my back doing some relaxing home improvements.
Was it weird painting a man on my lumbar region replete
with meat canister? Or was it fun? I am the world's
greatest DJ. I hold things aglue – like a guy weekend.
I hold a major salmon up for the camera it's fun. It's
bacon. The world is bacon wrapped around a scallop
to which I am allergic – no one thinks of that as surf
and turf but it is! Let's become cops and kiss.
That'll pass time. I took Metamucil before the damn
drag race. It was morning. Fun, as defined in Canada
is that what helps your movements. Headache.
I'm nearly dead with desire for a bike. Morgan
Freeman is voicing Visa ads up here and nobody
knows but me! I'm so different!

BATHURST TORONTO, 2010

Someone's breaking up with her boyfriend on this streetcar by phone.
"Clearly it's not working," she says. He concurs
by scream-sobbing on the other end.
A friend of mine once said,
"If you want to know the nature of a man,
staple a dollar into his pectoral muscle. Only a douchebag
would be pleased." That won't work here of course.
The dollars are all coins. The Queen is just a head,
demanded by the Baptist standing outside the LCBO
at Oakwood. Every dram of wine, he gets a tax.
Or doesn't. I'm American. I mail my dimes
to bums in Somerville, Mass. It's great,
minus the exchange rate. Now and then I slip
a TTC token in just to frustrate them.
A trinket 'bout as big as a bird monocle.
One day I will marry in a hail of transfer
tickets torn to bits by big children.

CHLOROFORM

Fat mannequins. God bless
the bastard who decided that. Every body rates
plaster. I want a mannequin of Earth.
All is sound. Round plump prow. Now,
a regular couple compares paunches.
Promising leisurely punches on cattle.
Calgary. The future's enormous
together. This giant country and its
belly of flowers. A meadow sidles
up and tackles your garden. Four grasshoppers
don't scare me as much as five. Saturated
cactus in aspic, O this caribou ablution.
Tomorrow – work. Right now – officially
no reason to remain thin.

THANKSGIVING IN AMERICA

Toronto is sad.
Manhattan is decoratively sad.
Chrissie Hynde is there, warning us
not to eat cocoa dipped with bees.
Heed her.
                    Boston

is purgatractive – one
Charlie Horse away from debtor's jail.
I am done. My tombstone
has forceps hanging off of it like former
ornaments. Canadian people ape Spanish over
average booze. And Washington, ah Washington is
empty of angels now. They're all
in Ohio – zuzshing the drapes of natal dreams.
Certain in luff.
Me: this tight cellar local.

COMMERCIAL BREAK – TORONTO

Let's, together, pump up your ham.
I'm talking about your calves.
                                          Food
is secret boob-touching.

"App" used to be short for "appetizer." Now,
Cold Metal America has succumbed to robot footsie.
I'm afraid to think for myself about doing you, so I present
a secret tray of peanut brittle.
That's my normal. I call it,
"going to my normal."

Right now a handshake and later a vampire
burning herself on the digital hearth: the "dearth."
I'm game. I'm galley.
I have yellow birds for gills, it's
okay though, all I do is rock the Xbox solo.
I bought this beanbag chair for 300 Canadian dollars
only to sit in a forest of one.

ONE TRAIN

> *In a poem, one line may hide another line,*
> *As at a crossing, one train may hide another train.*
> *That is, if you are waiting to cross*
> *The tracks, wait to do it for one moment at*
> *Least after the first train is gone. And so when you read*
> *Wait until you have read the next line—*
> *Then it is safe to go on reading.* –Kenneth Koch

Beware of Earth.

It might Pac Man you up like an obstinate
pizza with a piece plucked out of it.

One train becomes another train.

If you're traveling along the F line in Manhattan
there's a chance it'll suddenly turn into the C line. They'll say so
through the round drain in the ceiling
but it's too late. The change is made. One train
became a different one. Like your father becoming
some nameless passer-by at the corn emporium.
Same-ish, yes, but un-himly. The face
shivers your graveside that way, that's how it unfolds.

It wouldn't happen in Boston – the Red Line
doesn't change into the Green Line mid-
steam, humping you past two universities en route
to loveless nuptial. Nor in Chicago on the L. In Toronto
one subway line can't become another
'cause there's only two: a U bisected crossways
like the reticle in your weapon scope. One mind
becomes another mind in Canada after five months
living there and yet another near one year.
But you won't find a train or streetcar transforming
or the Dufferin bus with any number but 29
etched into its foreglass.

At night,
one wonders whether one wine has become another.
Neither should you open what with every
devil readying his morning might for you but still –
this Grenache is offish like a Tempranillo bought with cat food money.
One cat is another cat every minute we know from owning them.
Flirtatious turns acerbic as it works in love. Cats
are poor facsimiles for paramours we know from loneliness

but they're used for that. A cat transforms into other animals.
One moment a Komodo dragon the next a throw blanket.
Down is stuffed into my plastic history book to keep the past
from leaking out but it does anyway. One moment
becomes another moment when remembered.

One poet may impregnate another. It happened
in 1972 New York and again two years later. So that's
two poet brothers corsicannily swapping clothes
until the oldest sired a child with yet another poet.
Love might turn into another kind of love if you're careless.
The gushful lusty sort can grow
brotherly in a 12-year apartment. Either way you become
and unbecome each other in ways either completing or
boringly scary. "Put on a happy face" is a song.
"Put on my husband's face" is a nightmare –
or a movie in which Gwyneth Paltrow played Sylvia Path.
One woman became the other in that case although
the latter was dead. If you're an asshole, the Starbucks barista
will use whole milk for your triple mocha instead of skim.
Delicious, but a different beverage than you asked for.
"Asked for" meaning "ordered" not as in "you asked for it
asshole!" Don't confuse the two. You can be a Zionist
and not an observant Jew I learned in New Jersey. Nat
Nadler fought the British aboard the Exodus 1947 in 1947.
One nation can become another, it happened one year later.
One potater, two potater.

I get incensed when suddenly on the wrong
subway through no fault of my own and become someone else.
Someone who's forgotten he'll one day die
and a walk from West 4th Street won't hasten the process.
Someone muttering bits of this poem into an iPhone and who thus
records himself saying "no" to a homeless veteran begging
food money. Yes, one minute I'm that guy, the next
I'm someone marching back to the beggar
with an outstretched American bill. If you spare change
for a former marine he might transmogrify into a shyster drunk
before your eyes. Be careful.
He could curse your paltry dollar or,
God forbid, declare that you're a saint: shame

hugs your underpinnings.
You could use a blessing in this city
with its listing go-downs. Poop
of varying hues appointing the path
to 2nd Avenue F station where changes occur.

One night runs into another on this orange sofa dutifully
scrivening. Well, more bluish orange. More raspberry sherbet
than salmon floral bra I tried to palm off the body of the blondest
girl I ever saw at 14. O how boozelessly we wrimpled
under her sleeping bag. I forget what you want me to forget
until I'm home and then it blinks on like news.
One thing I should tell you about my belly is that it
used to be slippered. I know no dude should say so
to an audience but honest I was suppler.
Now every part of me slumbers in its turn. One limp
limb replaces another mid-Van Winkle.

The upstairs neighbors are fucking again, replacing
each other's fluids with their own. The "talk talk talk"
of lumber on lumber hangs me down like a dick-shaped clock.
My Canadian toaster tinks akin noises but isn't shtupping anyone.
An entire lack of shtupping occurs in this Bucharest.
Who is Neil Diamond to say "I Am I Said," he got
more backstage-action than the whole cast of "Oh! Calcutta!"
"Seen one you seen 'em all" goes the finale refrain when all
the actors doff their gear and fake screw. Great big yowling
"seen one" they all sum to. The parts were private.

I'm on a D train floating bridge level through apartment blocks.
Mini-gold proscenium proscenium proscenium like glowing teeth.
Aimed Southeast to Union I'll canter to Degraw and sit,
watch comedian comedian comedian tear their former suppliants
a fresh anus on stage. But then the D begins to roll
along the Q line. We're told so through ceiling drain.
The drift is much more Eastern than the hard hook
south I paid for, more slidden than certain. I stupidly stay put
because Brooklyn is Brooklyn but one Brooklyn
can become another.   Pop off at Lafayette,
double back to Fulton, there's no
platform squat to cop and scratch this down so I wait
three unlikely weeks 'til I'm on a couch in Chicago.

Snow here bangs my body like being shat
upon by a teeny vegan god.
Who's to say what train is fitter?
"I am," I say out loud to three blue
chairs, all empty. More green than blue.
More sea glass than cerulean, the masthead
of my delusive newspaper has three
deceased presidents in it, all interchangeable.
Who remembers which one Chester Arthur was anyway?
"I do," says Chester Arthur from beyond the urn.
A man who never happened
may have, but became fictive
by unmemory.

I counted. And if each
pack of additiveless cigarettes costs
14-dollars, and I buy one
every third day, that's $4.67 or so
per day, ergo, I am living
as a pack-a-day smoker in 1995.
My best friend's girl back then walked
into a liquor store for smokes on July 4th
and said, "Do you have American Spirit?" not realizing.

In the air from O'Hare to LaGuardia, a hole
in the deep clouds equals floating tundra volcano.
No danger do I foresee that we'll descend
into Logan, Pearson or Heathrow or,
for that matter, hell. It doesn't happen
up here. One plane stays itself
solitarily, a single ginger pearl tossed
angel to angel. On the ground
things may shift. One plane can replace
another if the first is late. They interchange.
On take off though, all anonymity
subsides – for planes and for their pulpating
contents. One of us is so obese
he carries a special seat belt extender.
The guy behind him? Alopecia. Yanks
a scrap of skin behind his ear and snacks on it.

Says "cookie" when the in-flight concession
basket comes around. Every baseball diamond
is a rare snowflake from above.

"Ladies and gentlemen once again because of construction
this Manhattan bound F train will run over the A Line.
The next stop on this train is High Street Brooklyn Bridge.
For service on the F line stay on this F train to West 4th
Washington Square Park and change back to a Brooklyn bound
F making all regular F stops by Rutgers Street Tunnel. Next stop
High Street Brooklyn Bridge, F train via the A by Cranberry Street
to West 4th Washington Square. Stand clear of the closing doors please."

Writing my accountant tonight I try to type "thanks so muchly"
but my iPhone corrects it to "thanks douchey." One sentiment
becomes its opposite that swiftly – just like this sentence
became about something other than Spiderman before you were aware.
The Spiderman is a burger at Bartley's in Harvard Square,
or was. The names change every year. The owners
think up new ones at a lake in New Hampshire. I'd tell you
this year's burger names but it'd date the poem past
what I already oh who gives a shit: there's "The Facebook,"
"The Joe Biden" and "The iPhone." In the Facebook movie,
two actors played twins but they weren't. One face
was CGI'd onto the other so that both were him. One scene
they sit in Bartley's eating burgers, don't know which ones.
That scene lasts 7 seconds.

One day becomes another every midnight. You often straddle
them; when's that mean you're waking, tomorrow or today?
At night it's morning in Switzerland and vice
versa. One of us drinks wine. The other's in pajamas, working.
One time I went to Spain but I was only dreaming. One dream
is like the rest, they're all my circadian stadium rioting.
One apartment is this apartment. Another's yours. They're
separated by 19,000 cruise-liners laid end to end.
One body can never absorb another. We all have waterproof
edges, itching, reading Epsom boxes produced in other countries.
In the end, one body becomes no body – a dim branch
planted like a prune pit and, God-willing, pondered.

CODA:

"The signals are against us."
I'm on a D train straining Brooklyn's easel.
No discernable ambulance. Ad-libbed
Saturday ambitions include cake with
Ben and Catrin in Flatbush.
"The signals are against us."

"The signals are against us," says the driver,
his churn is low. Motor December lurching
forward without idle. But here,
in early calendar, all is pause.
A girl and her hero giggle
over phone pictures.

"Why're my cheekbones so crazy?" she says.
"Baby," he says, "There's nothin' wrong with your cheekbones."
"The signals are against us."

"The signals are against us," says it every
station, Union, 4th Ave., Prospect. Both
my hands become bony puppets canoodling.
"Why're my cheekbones so crazy," one hand says.
"Baby," says the other, "you don't have cheekbones,
you're a hand." Nothing signifies an item like itself.
Days don't float to some hereafter they go underground.
Every evening bears a pall upon its bald branches.
Carriages may return, but carriage-returns never recur.
And it's not 'til miles pass this time around, 'til pinhole
dot at tunnel-end dissolves, that all my thoughts fuse
into one brown idea: I'm on a D train
but was s'posed to have boarded a B train
this evening. That's the line Ben lives on, the B.
"B" like Ben, or Brooklyn, or baby.
"B" like become, becoming, or became.

AMTRAK TO A MEMORIAL

for William Corbett

Thought about packing the half-
bottle of scotch but I'll be on two
morning trains. One
to Bill's hurrah. Not his last
I bet. I'd forgotten
morning becomes mid-
afternoon fast on a train.
No faster than a locomotive but
just as. And I will need that hooch
later when I hear Bill saying each
word aloud as I write it down.

Bill –
I got your rhythms in my mouth
this morning reading poems from
"Opening Day." Brave atlas
of proper names and browing
at seasons. I see you, face
windward, at some city river
or other. Or near pond.
It's never over. We're poets.
We can speak with the dead.

COMMERCIAL BREAK

Every day matters. Especially
when you're a beautiful woman
running through the plaza
with balloons.
We're all in this together. Some of us
are Dave Matthews, Tina Turner
and Gwyneth Paltrow.
This is America
where you can succeed if
you're already superlative.
I'm fat. (Inside.)
I pale under the hefty
thought of old cola.
Sky-writers riddle high blue.
The whole beach tries to push
my heart back to ocean. Soon
fucking Bono arrives.
Money snows from clouds.
I could scour the whole
parking lot and never find my car.
I drove Yo Yo Ma here.
He bored me with a world
of conversation about his awards.
We played Megadeth on the iPod.
Millionaire. Devil. A rose.
I'm sorry. The difficulty is
I'm bad at everything.
And to be surrounded by all
this seraphim – it itties you.
Once,
a talented man
yelled at me
for saying "itty."

Itty.

Sean Cole's previous poetry collections include *The December Project* (Boog Literature), *Itty City* (Pressed Wafer), and *One Train* (Dusie). His poems have also appeared in *The Brooklyn Rail*, *Court Green*, *Black Clock*, *Pavement Saw*, and *Boog City* among other journals, and in the anthology *Starting Today: 100 Poems for Obama's First 100 Days*. For more than 20 years, Cole has contributed stories to various public radio programs and podcasts including *Radiolab*, *99% Invisible*, *Studio 360*, and *All Things Considered*. He is currently a producer and occasional guest host of *This American Life*.

www.ingramcontent.com/pod-product-compliance
Lightning Source LLC
Chambersburg PA
CBHW042101120526
44592CB00026B/15